MW01624683
To
Sweet reading
Sweet listening

Shooggie's

MARSHMALLOW RAIN

Story by Pamela Ebert Davidson
Illustrations by Christine Danylik Ivers

A
Little Shooggie Book

LSB, Inc ♡ Ellington, Connecticut

Here's Shooggie

From his soft, purple toes
To his very pink nose,
He's oodles of fun,
All rolled into one.

He's cute.
He's sweet.
He's silly.
He's neat.

He's the one,
the only
Shooggie!

Hi Buddies!

Here's one of my favorite stories written just for you!

Hugs & Kisses,

Shooggie's Marshmallow Rain

For information, address LSB, Inc.
8 Punkin Drive, Ellington, CT 06029
First Edition
Printed in the United States of America

Printing by Davidson & McKirdy Co., Inc.
Binding by A. Horowitz & Sons

DAVIDSON, PAMELA EBERT
Shooggie's Marshmallow Rain
Summary: Shooggie fantasizes raindrops are
Marshmallows, but soon realizes the consequences.

[1. Marshmallows–Fiction 2. Rain–Fiction]
I. Title

ISBN 0-911033-00-9

Library of Congress Catalog Number: 82-83612

To
Clayton,
Katie,
Lynn,
Tricia
and Ashley (the original Shooggie)

I wanted to play outside today,

But the clouds all chased the sun away.

**The sky grew dark . . . oh,
what a shame.**

And soon it began to . . .

Rain, and

Rain, and

Shooggie

RAIN!!!

Those little drops of watery wet,
Wanted to spoil my fun I bet.

BUT. . .

**Wouldn't I be a lucky fellow,
If every drop were a big
MARSHMALLOW!**

**If every puddle,
from every drip,**

Were white and fluffy,
from tip to tip.

MARSHMALLOWS would stick,
to the bushes and trees.
I could nibble and gobble,
as much as I pleased.

**If it rained all day long,
more MARSHMALLOWS would fall.
They would seep through the windows,
and creep down the hall.**

They would fill all the rooms,
the doorways,
the stairs. . . .

White, fluffy MARSHMALLOWS everyplace . . .

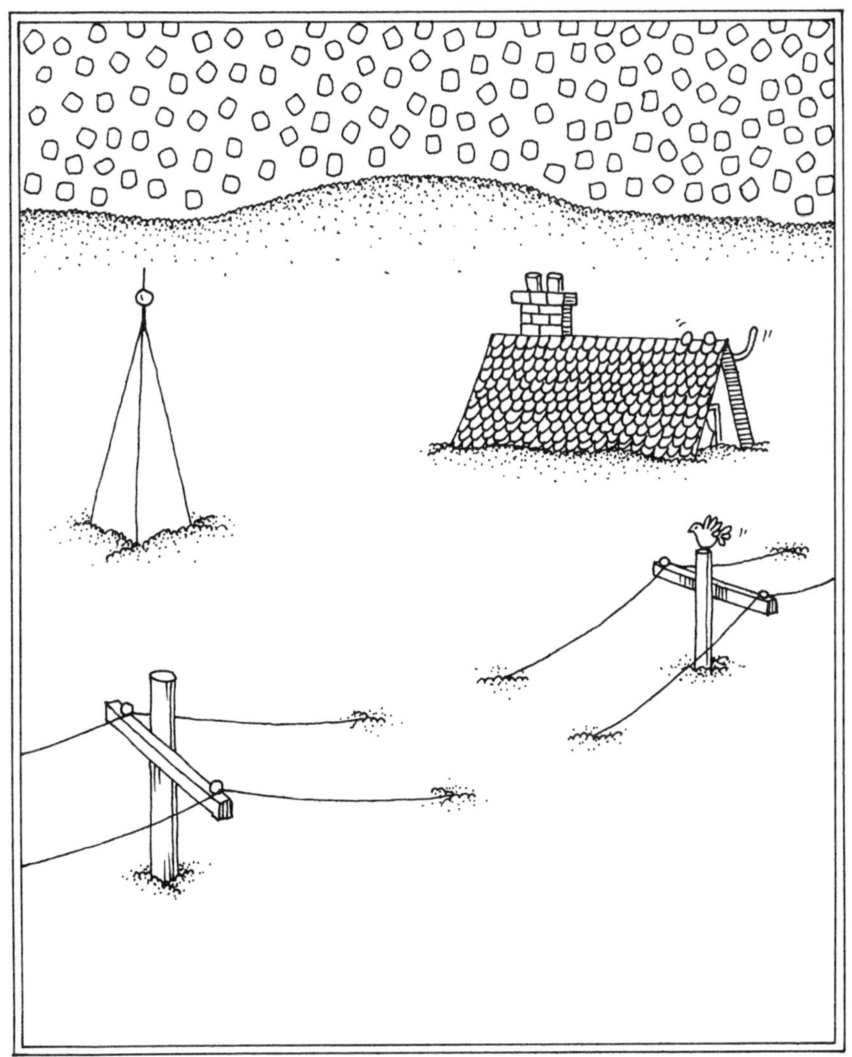

EVERYWHERE!

A MARSHMALLOW rain could be
oodles of fun,
But what if it stops and back comes
the sun?
Those MARSHMALLOWS would melt
and start to get sticky.

And all would be YUCKY and ICKY and YICKY ! ! !

My flowers all covered
with MARSHMALLOW goo,
Would droop to the ground
crying sticky . . .

BOO-HOOS!!!

BUT . . .

Shooggie

Look at the sky,
It stopped raining,
YIPPEE!
I can go out and play.
I can swing in my
Tree.

So, when drops start to fall,
it's not really a shame.
Close your eyes and pretend
it's a MARSHMALLOW RAIN.